Turtle Light Press Haiku Chapbook Contest Winners

Furrows of Snow, Glenn G. Coats (2019)

The Deep End of the Sky, Chad Lee Robinson (2015)

The Window That Closes, Graham High (2013)

All That Remains, Catherine J.S. Lee (2011)

Sketches from the San Joaquin, Michael McClintock (2009)

&

Other Turtle Light Press Haiku Books

Nick Virgilio: A Life in Haiku, Nick Virgilio
(Edited by Raffael de Gruttola)

Peace and War: A Collection of Haiku from Israel, Rick Black

Also by Rick Black

ARTIST BOOKS

Akedah: The Binding of Yitzhak, 2023

The Amichai Windows, 2017

Peace and War: A Collection of Haiku from Israel, 2007

Highland Park Centennial Album, 2005

POETRY

Star of David, 2013

Peace and War: A Collection of Haiku from Israel, 2007

ക

Two Seasons in Israel

Two Seasons in Israel

A Selection of Peace and War Haiku

Rick Black

Turtle Light Press • Arlington, Va. • 2024

For Mellie—may you find peace and strength on the road ahead.

Table of Contents

Introduction   i

Haiku
I. A Succulent Takes Refuge   1

II. The Nightmare of Battle   31

III. My Brother's Prayer Slip   55

IV. Blind Alleyway   81

V. Birds-of-Paradise   105

Glossary   132

Photo Credits   134

About the Author

Acknowledgments

Colophon

Introduction
By Rick Black

Israel is both a beautiful and violent land. I learned that during my six years living there, three of which I spent as a reporter in the Jerusalem bureau of *The New York Times*. I covered Palestinian demonstrations and the first Persian Gulf war, the arrival of Russian and Ethiopian Jewish immigrants and the founding of new Israeli settlements. I was often struck by the sharp contrasts of the country: Palestinians and Jews, the Negev and the Galilee, ancient and modern. Although I wanted to write about the country in a deeper way, to plumb its paradoxes and contradictions, I was limited by the parameters of the newspaper trade and its vocabulary. I was largely restricted to filing stories about war, demonstrations and terrorist attacks.

In 1992, when I returned to the States, I received a book about haiku—those tiny, imagistic poems that last so briefly but make an abiding impression like a firefly in the night. I loved their short, concise form and non-judgmental approach to the world. I began to read and learn more about haiku. In particular, I was struck by the poems of Nick Virgilio, a haiku poet who used the genre to deal with the death of his youngest brother in Vietnam.

deep in rank grass,
through a bullet-riddled helmet:
an unknown flower
               Nick Virgilio

Reading Virgilio's poems, I realized that haiku might help sort out the contradictory emotions that Israel evoked in me. I started to write a lot of haiku and won several awards. When I returned to Israel a few years later, I jotted down some possible poems, thoughts and impressions. I strove to make connections between olive trees and refugee camps, military cemeteries and blossoming rosemary, great blue herons and F-16s in a way that I had always wanted to but was never able to do as a reporter. I wrote about the stark images of Israel's landscape—images of peace and war, of hope and fear—and the way in which they blended together. I discovered haiku in the shattered remains scattered around the country; I found them in Jerusalem's alleyways and Galilee's orchards, at war memorials and religious shrines. I found them, in fact, hiding everywhere like thistles amid rocky outcroppings.

highway's edge—
old armored vehicles rust
beneath cypress trees

A poetic form that developed in Japan in the 17th century, haiku are most often written in three lines and a total of 17 syllables or fewer in English. They are meant to depict a specific moment in the present tense and to have some reference, direct or indirect, to nature. While many Japanese haiku reflect Zen teachings, they are not didactic and do not try to instill anything explicitly. The poems do, however, teach us about life; they reveal life itself to us in their own quiet way. "Haiku is a kind of satori, or enlightenment, in which 'we see into the life of things,'" writes R.H. Blyth in volume one of his classic four-volume work, *Haiku*. "We grasp the inexpressible meaning of some quite ordinary thing or fact hitherto over-looked." He continues: "Haiku record what Wordsworth calls those 'spots of time,' those moments which for some quite mysterious reason have a peculiar significance. There is a unique quality about the poet's state of feeling on these occasions; it may be very deep, it may be rather shallow, but there is a 'something' about the external things, a 'something' about the inner mind which is unmistakable." As Blyth says, haiku are not meant to be simply pictorial or decorative; they often incorporate the cruelty of nature. An example of this type of haiku can be found below in a poem written by one of the three great Japanese haiku masters:

The flying squirrel
is crunching the small bird
on the withered moor.
                    Yosa Buson

This haiku depicts a moment that was particularly significant to Buson, and he focuses on the intensity and immediacy of it. Not only is the bird doomed but the moor has withered. Life itself is ending—and so will our own one day. But, by re-maining indirect, by finding an external image for his internal feelings, Buson evokes a sense of mystery that expands beyond the poem itself. By doing so, he manages to imprint the haiku moment in our own minds.

After my return from Israel, I sat at my desk each morning with my notebook and pencil. I recopied the poems—or intimations of poems—onto a sheet of paper, and then tried to listen to the words. A flood of sunlight often slanted into my study. I had to lower the window blinds to keep the sun's glare out of my eyes. Sometimes I paused to gaze up at a mourning dove nestled in the crook of a fig tree whose branches scraped against the window pane in the breeze. A prickly pear cactus grew beneath another window, reminding me of the Arab women who roamed through Jerusalem's neighborhoods, shouting, "Sabras, sabras!" with their cardboard cartons of sweet, juicy cactus fruit atop their heads. Surrounded by maps of Israel and Jerusalem, a poster by Marc Chagall entitled, "Paris View," books in Hebrew and English, and photos of the snow-covered yard of my childhood home in New Jersey, I allowed each haiku to transport me back to Israel. Sometimes I left the original version alone; at other times, I reworked it over and over as if using a mortar and pestle to grind hummus.

Ironically, the smallness of haiku quite aptly mirrors the tiny size of Israel. Perhaps one could say that haiku more appropriately reflect "the still, small voice" of the Biblical landscape than that of the vast American wilderness. The brevity of haiku invites a plethora of interpretations; the gaps allow readers to fill in the meanings of the poems in terms of their own experience. Of course, haiku in the English-speaking world will never be identical to Japanese haiku. We write in a different language and cultural milieu; we can approach the Japanese form and sensibility, but that is as close as we will ever get—or ever should. Our language, cultural references, and audience all affect the style, content, meaning and interpretation. While haiku emerged out of a Japanese literary tradition, though, there is no reason why we cannot borrow the form and use it in English just as a sonnet does not have to be written solely in Italian. Each genre is defined in terms of its own poetic form and sensibility, not geographic space.

In fact, many North American haiku poets have experimented quite drastically, trying to stretch the limits of the form as much as possible. Some write haiku in one line (*in spite of everything...forsythia* by Peggy Willis Lyles) while others use vertical lines of poetry.

at
the
deep
end
of
the
sky
prairie
    Chad Lee Robinson

I tend to remain faithful to the three-line poetic form, but I often depart from a 5-7-5 syllable count in order to convey the poem's essence as concisely as possible in English. The core of each of my haiku resides in the tension between people and their surroundings or nature. The Zen-ness, the sense of wonder and awe, is created through a sense of paradox, contradiction, or internal comparison. I strive to capture a specific moment in time as well as the emotional layers of meaning and context that resonate within it. To achieve my effect, I purposely tap literary associations, cultural and religious traditions, and words in English, Hebrew and Arabic to connect the striated layers of time that I sense so deeply and palpably in Israel. In doing so, I attempt to intermingle echoes of the past and future within the narrow confines of haiku.

1918 cemetery
an olive tree's new branches
shoot towards the sky

Like many post-World-War-II Japanese haiku poets, I am impatient with only writing about natural beauty in and of itself. I particularly enjoy experimenting with the interplay of the natural and human worlds, and often my poems are located at the intersection between the two. I believe that nature can also be used ironically. Like Tomizawa Kakio, an unconventional post-World-War-II Japanese haiku poet, I enjoy contrasting human and natural phenomena, as he does in this haiku below:

An aged seagull
Over waters where a warship foundered.
                              Tomizawa Kakio

Whether in Tokyo or Jerusalem, Kyiv or New York, haiku can and should depict the modern age and even incorporate images of missiles, tanks and other military weapons. It needs to deal with the realities of the 21st century. I deeply admire poets like Saito Sanki, a contemporary of Tomizawa who tried to deal with the horrific effects of war in Japan. In 1947, he penned this haiku:

Starving, how friendly
everyone is! The autumn wind
comes from the distance.
                              Saito Sanki

In another, he tried to deal with the aftermath of Hiroshima in his homeland. How could as delicate and short a poem as a haiku be used to reflect such an enormous, terrifying reality? Yet, he found a way to do it in a poem that later became quite well known:

At Hiroshima
when I eat a boiled egg
I open my mouth.
          Saito Sanki

It is a lot to ask of such a short poem. Haiku have often been criticized for being too short—either inadequate to express complex realities or puerile because of their deceptive simplicity. The importance of a poem or a word, though, does not depend on its length but on its resonance. Through haiku, we can pass on our impressions to others like a fragile glass of wine and say: "Here, drink! Savor this moment, too!" For savoring the here and now, appreciating the "being-ness" of each thing, looking at the world in all its detail is what haiku have taught me.

desert fortress:
a succulent takes refuge
in its ruins

Nonetheless, I struggle to reconcile haiku's non-judgmental approach to life with my own deep-seated need to protest against life's injustice. I suppose that I have an ongoing argument with God about the world's imperfections—about people's cruelty to each other as well as nature's cruelty and seeming indifference to us. Simply to accept the world as it is, as Zen philosophy requires, does not come naturally to me. I have always found it difficult to accept a Japanese poetic form whose philosophical underpinnings contradict my Jewish sensibility. Yet, if it is a protest that I want to lodge, perhaps haiku is not the right place for it. Or, perhaps I should say, not the right form for it. Donald Keene, a Japanese literary historian, writes in a Japanese literary history, *Dawn to the West*, that "it is unlikely that the haiku can ever be the most effective form a writer can use to convey his indignation over, say, a political system that tolerates the terrible working conditions in the salt fields. An indictment in some other form—whether of journalism, fiction or modern poetry—would certainly be more likely to produce a strong effect."

In a certain sense, haiku have forced me to put aside my own sense of life's injustice. There are times to protest against life and times to accept it—and one needs to learn to distinguish between them. It is not always easy to accept life with a sense of grace. As Blyth writes, "When we are grasping the inexpressible meaning of these things, this is life, this is living. To do this twenty-four hours a day is the Way of Haiku. It is having life more abundantly." Most of the time, though, I cannot live so fully. I still feel compelled to protest against God's inscrutable ways in the universe. By writing haiku, though, I have found a way to put aside my protest for at least a few minutes each day and to savor life in all its mystery.

In 2007, I published a small, handmade dos-a-dos artist book with some of my haiku: *Peace and War: A Collection of Haiku From Israel*. On one side, I placed poems primarily about peace; on the other, mostly about war. All of them were linked together, as these two are in daily life in Israel, by a single binding. But dozens of poems never made it into the collection. They remained in my drawer—silent witnesses of a torn country.

With the massacre of Israelis on October 7 and the subsequent war in the Gaza Strip, I finally realized that I needed to share the rest of these poems, so I reworked many of them from their original form or publications where they had appeared. The difficulty, as it has always been for me, was how to organize them into a collection. By geographic region, by natural seasons or by other factors? Ultimately, I realized that the poems were divided between two seasons: peace and war. In fact, these are the main seasons of life in Israel.

In organizing this collection of haiku, I have tried to create a sense of synergy by using an associative method of switching back and forth between images of peace and war. Sometimes, I group poems together in similar geographic regions, other times I connect natural season poems. But it is always with the idea of alternating poems of peace and war in the flow of the book. From one day to the next, one simply never knows what to expect.

Can one find beauty in a land so laden with violence? A land riveted by war yet striving for peace? Indeed, one can—perhaps one must. Despite their brevity, haiku are able to convey a deep sense of the land of Israel and the people who are caught in its heartrending complexities. Haiku can help us to focus on and treasure the "little" things in life and cherish the time, however brief it is, that we have together.

last clouds—
if only the violence would
drift away, too

৵

I. A Succulent Takes Refuge

so far away
from this country's strife
desert stars

a butterfly
lost in the sandstorm
Makhtesh Ramon

a Bedouin bikes
past infantry tanks
Negev exercises

listening to shells
by the edge of the Galilee—
distant explosions

just the two of us
driving along the border
in the dark

no sons left—
just a rose garden planted
in their memory

lengthening shadows
my loneliness deepens
at dusk

luggage repair—
if only our broken hearts
could be mended

in Jerusalem,
even the people are
covered by dust

pockmarked wall:
bullet shells still lodged
deep within

counting the rings
of the pine's stump—
its share of war

billboard flaking
in the Mediterranean sun—
paper baklava

by the ramparts,
red *callaniot* flutter
so briefly

winter drought
the land's rebellion
against zealots

late rose—
all but one petal
blown away

desert fortress:
a succulent takes refuge
in its ruins

Ein Gedi preserve
closes early for Shabbat—
ibex still feeding

heat lightning
the voices of children
still at play

Hasidic boys
slide down the bomb shelter—
its slippery roof

Mea Shearim
glass menorahs mirror
flickering stars

quiet again
at the war memorial—
forgotten dreidel

sound asleep
in his father's arms—
to be drafted, too?

an armored tank
completely surrounded:
queen anne's lace

near the battlefield,
fresh olive trees planted
row after row

Wailing Wall
my sorrow so quickly
turns to stone

she kisses me
while I'm reading Isaiah—
September morning

in rapid fire,
alto sax notes climb
over the ramparts

all the anemones—
if only peace would spread
through the valleys

snowy egrets:
at least there's a refuge
to protect them

Hula swamp
a cormorant preens itself
in still waters

beyond sorrow
above the distant shoreline . . .
herring gulls dive

soldier's burial
Taps fade slowly
into silence

old friends
warm pita and za'atar
together again

still asleep:
the warmth of her breasts
against me

no dogwood trees
in the Jerusalem hills—
missing you, too

red poppies—
how they just appear
on the hillsides

piano concerto:
hear it coming from
the bomb shelter?

pristine sky:
the dead of the Great War
and those yet to come

no air raid sirens—
just a seesaw creaking
in the night

cumulus clouds
drift past the cemetery . . .
World War I

despite the gunfire,
white water lilies open—
Easter morning

empty bunker:
spying a Hasidic couple
and their kids

a Franciscan monk
talking on his cell phone—
his flowing robe

sign posted
at the Latrun monastery:
"Don't hurt the flowers!"

II. The Nightmare of Battle

pink bougainvillea:
does the enemy admire
its blossoms, too?

Old City
shiny barbed wire,
spirals of fear

a toddler
watches TV alone—
more wounded

in silence,
the ancient hills do
bow down

Remembrance Day:
sipping a cup of strong tea
in his memory
for Ben

freshly dug graves—
the Arab gravedigger
kneels to pray

partly uprooted—
a bulldozed olive tree
still in bloom

melting clockfaces
of a Dali painting
drip irrigation

just an olive tree
and a peeling mural left
Yitzhak Rabin square

echo of their boots—
German tourists trod through
the Jewish Quarter

bicycle cart:
peddling sesame rolls
by Jaffa Gate

clay shards
in the souvenir shop
shattered dreams

a soldier relives
the nightmare of battle—
Tel Aviv beachfront

red hibiscus
by Galilee's edge . . .
falling in love

pomegranate—
its bloodshot kernels
glistening

Christmas Eve:
bells upon bells
late at night

a monk's sandals—
down the same stairwell,
a soldier's boots

Negev boot camp
soldiers on stretchers fake
being wounded

your rejoicing
is premature, fireworks—
no messiah yet

empty sandbox—
a mortar shell explodes
harmlessly nearby

a discarded doll
stares at the Judean desert
so vacantly

after the sirens,
the sound of children
playing hopscotch

flies swarm
the iced sea bream
summer dreams

a vendor shouts
loudly to customers:
"Sweet watermelon!"

inhaling the scent
of mounds of za'atar—
Tel Aviv *shuk*

Jewish Quarter
an Orthodox girl loosens
her black braids

a rainbow arcs
above the domed rooftops,
still glistening

a little extra
for the blind customer—
sesame halvah

one-legged vet:
the ricochet of dice
by his espresso

at half-mast,
a faded flag flutters
for the fallen

jasmine's aroma—
yet the war is coming,
coming soon

by ancient roots,
the spent cartridges and
olive pits

great blue herons
heading south like F-16s—
autumn maneuvers

rock doves
flirting by the soldier's grave
so joyously

sergeant's orders—
soldiers cock their rifles
at the azure sky

night sky
another checkpoint
or a star?

not yet abloom . . .
pink geraniums planted
in army boots

spring picnic:
by old command headquarters,
forgotten battles

just buried soldier—
too soon for his mother
to notice the crocus

גן
מואל

III. My Brother's Prayer Slip

Ammunition Hill
pink tea roses blossom
at its bottom

a soldier's Uzi
targets the Beatles poster
above his bed

bits of masking tape
stuck to the windowpane—
Gulf War remnants

white geranium
on the terrace of my flat—
who lives there now?

three homeless
asleep by the pink roses
Liberty Bell park

Dome of the Rock
three red poppies
by its entrance

impossible
to see all the gravestones—
Mount of Olives

desert cliffs
a single cloud's
shadow

rainy season—
Dead Sea juice stands
boarded up

border lookout—
the flamingos in flight
to and fro

salt marshes
the sound of wings
in silence

listening keenly:
how many air raid sirens
tonight?

his fatigues drying
in the sunlight—
soldier asleep

Western Wall
my brother's prayer slip
next to mine
for B.

plowshares, indeed—
will we ever stop
waging war?

soldier's grave—
lovers' initials carved
so nearby

above the bloodstains,
pink oleanders arc
haphazardly

a bulbul hiding
in the pomegranate—
too shy to sing

off the Kinneret,
warm breezes strum
the date palms

engraved guitar
plays the *hamsin's* song
Negev cemetery

perfectly
still in the *hamsin*—
wooden egret

Nabatean ruins
a few tourists stop in
the living room

Russian accordionist
longingly sings of elsewhere—
Mitzpeh Ramon

DP camp photo:
more than four questions
at our seder

just after Pesach,
the scent of revenge
in the night

dark, celestial sky—
even the doves mourn
the dead

late winter eve
lugging a sack of kittens
past the *shuk*
               for Father Michael Doyle

Hasidic kids
close to the popcorn maker:
late Hanukkah eve

empty bench:
flies feed off challah
left for beggars

Two Seasons in Israel

laundry line—
three prayer shawls *daven*
in the breeze

no snow yet
on the domed rooftops—
Christmas Eve

Wailing Wall—
a cabbie complains loudly
about politics

a capella
deep-voiced monks and
mourning doves

ancient dig—
a jackhammer echoes
distant hills

Sea of Galilee:
orange trumpet vines
walk on water

reading a book,
In Search of God
Mea Shearim

looking up
at the evening stars—
not one missing

harvest moon
the yeshiva boys play
hide-and-seek

Jerusalem sky—
no chariots of fire today,
just spring clouds

upside-down
from the monkey bars:
crosses and domes

triplets fast asleep:
the scent of baby powder
in the bomb shelter

Shabbat eve—
the angels of peace
frightened away

IV. Blind Alleyway

1918 cemetery
young olive branches shoot
towards the sky

polished shoes
during the memorial service:
perfectly still

all these swords . . .
when will they turn
to dust?

bumper sticker
by the war memorial:
A Time to Love

red poppies:
as if they'll be there
forever

after lovemaking,
sipping the mint tea—
its sweetness

for L.

the wings of the dove—
how faultless they seem
in the sunlight

a towhee dances
on its injured foot
klezmer music

September eve:
raindrops tap dance
across the stage

rattling loudly—
honey locust seedpods
in the Negev

Beersheva bakery:
the aroma of fresh pita
in sun-baked streets

Arab flea market:
a Jewish spice box
for sale

arched window—
a large *hamsa* hangs
by her crib

Arab and Jew
walk past each other:
blind alleyway

her aged hands
harvesting the olives
yet again

ripening figs . . .
so quickly the generations
come and go

last clouds
if only the violence
would drift away, too

awakening
in the bomb shelter—
is it safe yet?

highway's edge
old armored vehicles rust
beneath cypress trees

scattered straw
in a neglected field
fallen soldier

last sunlight
on the gilded parapets—
faded dreams

bright oranges tilt
its tarnished weights:
rusty scale

Muslim Quarter:
boys keep playing soccer
despite the gunshots

rusted howitzer:
still targeting a pine
and its crows

Christmas Eve:
the echo of gunfire
in the alleyway

olive tree
a black cat sharpens
its claws

almond blossoms—
long before I'm here,
long after

Ammunition Hill
the cold, slanting rain pierces
hollowed-out rocks

unknown blossoms:
purple, white and pink
to ease her grief

oleander blooms
and the waves breaking ashore . . .
may they never cease
                 for Hannah Senesh

old veterans
revisit the battlefield
arm-in-arm

my first war—
how this rustling pine
still calms me

sunflower . . .
remembering her son,
lost in battle

ashlar stones
paper prayer slips
fallen

olive trees—
their tiny, yellow blossoms,
promise of fruit

V. Birds-of-Paradise

smashed Arab gravestones:
wild caper blossoms
go rampant

not yet dawn
the sound of a muezzin's call
and disco music

oil lamps—
their holiness slowly
tapers out

diesel smoke—
the dark stone buildings
exhausted

wintry gust
the ashes of prayer slips
rise up

Rambam's tomb
a young woman's prayers
to get pregnant

by Haifa Bay,
hawking birds-of-paradise
for Shabbat

just tomcats
on patrol in the alleyway . . .
no one else

so tired—
a Palestinian berates
the red berets

mourning doves
arc through the Holy Sepulchre—
early pilgrimage

purple bougainvillea
beyond the barbed wire
flowering wildly

olive tree:
its roots clinging so
stubbornly

Herod's tomb—
rolling down the hill,
over and over

Two Seasons in Israel

Jewish Quarter
on her father's shoulders,
a piggyback ride

Armenian Quarter
the shadows of girls
jumping rope

just traipsing
along the cobblestones,
glad to be alive

sudden gust—
long black dresses
lifted up

tzedaka box—
they donate daily
to my heart
        for Mellie

at the bus stop,
she recites psalms
patiently

on the car,
a bumper sticker:
Psalms vs. Missiles

all the sanderlings
retreating from the waves—
jet fighters

coming harvest:
an orange grove beneath
weightless clouds

McDonald's arches
where convoys perished
in 1948

a land of walls—
the climbing geraniums
ignore them

his buddy's shoulder—
young soldier scribbles
a prayer slip

reading the eulogy
to convince himself
yet again

in vain
the milkweed stalks . . .
seeking butterflies

by the footstone,
her deaf son's *kaddish*
fades away

after her death,
the olive tree still
unharvested

so frail—
the friar's hands lifted
in blessing

holy land—
pissing on the bark
of a cypress

atop Mt. Zion,
a *minyan* of crows
at dawn

at the *kotel*,
a sea of black hats
ebbs and flows

Armenian museum:
a map of their genocide
graffitied over

dancing a *hora* . . .
his grandfather's gun handle
glistens brightly

sidewalk bloodstains—
pink oleanders arc
wildly

on the bus
ride a *keffiyeh*, a *streimel*
and a baseball cap

the beggar's eyes
this Christmas morning:
Via Dolorosa

on Shabbat,
even more delicate—
rockrose fragrance

dancing with her
at the edge of the desert—
is it a dream?

who brings out
rose bud after rose bud
in the spring?

barbed wire—
a calico cat lithely
slips past

spring *hamsin:*
only a few wildflowers
so far

Glossary

Ammunition Hill — The site of a battle in the Six-Day War between Israeli and Jordanian troops.

Armenian Quarter — One of four quarters of Jerusalem's Old City. The others are the Jewish, Muslim and Christian quarters.

Callaniot — The Hebrew word for poppies.

Dome of the Rock — An Islamic shrine at the center of the Al-Aqsa mosque compound.

Ein Gedi — An oasis in the Judean desert.

Hamsa — A good luck charm shaped like a hand.

Hamsin — An Arabic word for a hot, dry wind from the desert.

Herod — A Roman-appointed king of Judea known for his colossal building projects.

Holy Sepulchre — A church that is believed to mark the place of the crucifixion of Jesus and his burial tomb.

Hora — An Israeli circle dance.

Keffiyeh — An Arabic word for the traditional headdress worn by many men in the Middle East.

Kinneret — The name for the Sea of Galilee in Hebrew whose meaning is harp.

Kotel — The Hebrew word for the Wailing/Western Wall, a remnant of King Solomon's temple.

Liberty Bell Park — A park outside the Old City of Jerusalem.

Mahaneh Yehuda — An outdoor marketplace in Jerusalem.

Mahktesh Ramon — The largest canyon in the Negev desert.

Mitzpeh Ramon — A small town on the edge of the canyon.

Mea Shearim — A Hasidic neighborhood of Jerusalem.

Mount of Olives — A mountain topped with graves in Jerusalem, where the Messiah is supposed to first appear.

Mount Zion — A hill next to the Old City.

Nabatea — A Nabatean kingdom with ruins in the Negev desert.

Negev — A desert in southern Israel.

Rambam — A revered Sephardic Jewish scholar, philosopher and physician also known as Maimonides.

Shuk — The Hebrew word for marketplace.

Streimel — A fur hat worn by many Hasidic men.

Tzipori — An archeological park in central Galilee.

Tzedaka box — A box for anonymous charitable donations.

Yad Vashem — Israel's main memorial to the Holocaust.

Photo Credits

Cover photo taken by and reproduced courtesy of Rina Castelnuovo. Other photos listed below were taken by Rick Black unless otherwise noted.

Thistles scattered throughout the book.

Title Page — Alleyway in Jerusalem's Old City.

p. 4 — The windows in the YMCA tower overlooking the Old City from the western side.

p. 11 — A photo of a puppeteer mural in Tel Aviv taken by and reproduced courtesy of Bruce Black.

p. 18 — Hula Valley photo by the American Colony Photo Department reproduced courtesy of the Library of Congress.

p. 29 — The Dormition Abbey steeple and flowers in Jerusalem.

p. 36 — The Peaceland Bazaar in East Jerusalem near the Old City.

p. 42-43 — Abandoned buildings with stone arches on Jaffa Road in Jerusalem.

p. 53 — A memorial garden in the Yemin Moshe neighborhood of Jerusalem.

p. 60-61 — Papyrus reeds in the Hula Valley Nature Reserve. Photograph taken by Saar Yaacov and reproduced courtesy of the National Photo Archive of Israel.

p. 61 – A great blue heron captured by Meredith Blaché and reproduced courtesy of www.istockphoto.com.

p. 68 – Funeral notices in a Hasidic neighborhood.

p.79 – Large charity boxes affixed to buildings near the Mahane Yehuda marketplace in religious neighborhoods in Jerusalem.

p. 87 – A letter sent via the Hebrew postal service reproduced courtesy of Alex Ben-Arieh from the website, www.historama.com.

p. 90 – Clouds above the salt marshes north of Eilat.

p. 103 – Israeli women cadets at the Western Wall in the Old City.

p. 110 – A dove at the Western Wall photographed by Mikhail Levit and reproduced both here and on the cover courtesy of www.istockphoto.com.

p. 115 – A museum dedicated to art about the Psalms in Jerusalem.

p. 129 – Ein Gedi Nature Reserve photographed by Ludvig14 and reproduced courtesy of Wikimedia Commons.

Colophon – Fig leaf photo by the American Colony Photo Department reproduced courtesy of the Library of Congress.

About the Author

An award-winning book artist and poet, Rick Black lived in Israel for six years. He did post-graduate work in Hebrew literature at The Hebrew University in Jerusalem and subsequently worked as a journalist in the Jerusalem bureau of *The New York Times*.

After covering the first *intifada* and the first Persian Gulf war as well as other stories, Rick returned to the States. While he enjoyed journalism, he was intent on pursuing his love of literature and books.

By chance one day he discovered the Center for Book Arts in New York City and started taking classes. He won a fellowship there to attend a letterpress printing and fine press publishing seminar. After a class in miniature books with master book artist Maria Pisano, he was inspired to make a miniature dos-a-dos book of his own poems about his time in Israel, entitled *Peace and War: A Collection of Haiku from Israel*.

More recently, Rick's free verse collection, *Star of David*, won Poetica Magazine's poetry chapbook contest for contemporary Jewish writing and was named one of the best poetry books by Split This Rock in 2013.

In 2017, Rick completed *The Amichai Windows*, a ten-year project of translation, research, design, letterpress printing and hand bookbinding. A limited edition of 18 poems by renowned Israeli poet Yehuda Amichai, *The Amichai Windows* opens a window onto love, war, and being Jewish today.

In 2023, Rick published *Akedah: The Binding of Yitzhak*, an artist book that deals with the Biblical story of Abraham being commanded to sacrifice his beloved son, Isaac. An accordion book that stretches up to 50 feet, it was produced in a limited edition of eight copies.

Rick's artist books have been collected by numerous institutions, including the Rare Books Division of The Library of Congress, the Beinecke Rare Book and Manuscript Library of Yale University, the U.S. Holocaust Memorial Museum, the University of Michigan, the University of California at Berkeley, Rutgers University and others.

His honors also include the 2019 Isaac Anolic Jewish Book Arts Award and numerous haiku prizes in the U.S., Britain and Canada. His poems and translations have appeared in *The Atlanta Review*, *Midstream*, *U.S. 1 Worksheets*, *Frogpond*, *Cricket*, *Raw Nervz*, *Blithe Spirit*, *The Heron's Nest* and other journals.

A New Jersey native, he now lives in Arlington, VA, with his wife, Laura. He works out of Pyramid Atlantic Art Center in Hyattsville, MD.

ℚ

Acknowledgments

I am grateful to the editors of the following publications where some of these poems, or versions of them, first appeared: *Acorn, Blithe Spirit, Cricket, Frogpond, The Heron's Nest, Midstream, Raw Nervz, Simply Haiku, U.S. 1 Worksheets* and other journals. I am also appreciative to Haiku Canada for publishing an early worksheet of poems from Israel.

An earlier version of the introduction entitled, "Beauty and Violence in Israel," appeared in the 2016 anthology, *Deep Beauty* as well as in the British haiku journal, *Blithe Spirit*, in 2019.

About two dozen of these poems appeared in my dos-à-dos artist book *Peace and War: A Collection of Haiku from Israel.* published in 2007. I'd like to thank Kwame Dawes for reading first drafts of many of these poems as well as Penny Harter for her expertise and helpful suggestions.

I first discovered haiku thanks to my brother who gave me a copy of *The Haiku Handbook,* by William J. "Bill" Higginson and Penny Harter. Special thanks must also go to Nick Virgilio, whose elegiac poems about his brother's death in Vietnam made me realize that I could use the form for my own personal experiences of war and peace in Israel.

Of course, none of this work would have been possible without the love and support of my wife, Laura. She was the one who encouraged me even when it was hard to find the right words. Lastly, I dedicate this book to Mellie, who has brought me so much joy.

Colophon

So many years have gone by—and still war is a daily part of life in the Middle East. Hopefully, one day soon these poems will become a relic of the Israeli-Palestinian conflict, a witness to years of suffering that have long ended.

The cover photo of an Arab and Jew passing each other in an Old City alleyway was taken by and reproduced courtesy of Rina Castelnuovo, who worked together with Rick at *The New York Times* in Israel.

A dove at the Western Wall was photographed by Mikhail Levit and used with the permission of www.istockphoto.com. The thistles on the cover were taken by the author.

The cover font is Charlemagne Standard and the poem on the back cover is in Twentieth Century Condensed. The body of this book and poems are set in Goudy Old Style.

May 2024
Arlington, Virginia